A SHOPPING LIST
OF MYSTERY CLASSICS

by Pamela Granovetter
and Karen Thomas McCallum

Published by
The Copperfield Press
New York City, New York

Cover designed by
The Moorgate Group

Cover illustration courtesy of the
Trustees of the Boston Public Library

Copyright 1986 by The Copperfield Press

All rights reserved. No part of this book may be reproduced in any form without the permission of The Copperfield Press.

Printed in the United States of America

The Copperfield Press
306 West 11th Street
New York City, New York 10014

ISBN 0-9617037-0-9

First Edition

Introduction

The Copperfield collection of 609 classic works of crime, mystery and detection (published through 1950) has been compiled to assist you in shopping for and keeping track of books you want for your own home library. You will no longer have to bother with scraps of paper, index cards or notebooks. We have provided plenty of room for your own additional choices. Many of the titles suggested are out of print or difficult to find, but we have included an appendix of bookstores which carry newly reprinted or used classics. To help you avoid buying duplicates we have listed all alternate titles used in the United States or in England. For those of you new to this genre, there is an appendix of 25 easy-to-find favorites selected from the general list to get you started.

You can locate each shopping department as follows:

```
Classics . . . . . . . . . . . . . .  5 - 66
Bookstores . . . . . . . . . . . .  68 - 82
25 Favorites . . . . . . . . . . .  84 - 86
Special Bonus  . . . . . . . . .   88 - 95
```

HAPPY SHOPPING!

Pamela Granovetter
Karen Thomas McCallum

New York City, 1986

Books I:
Have
Read Want Own

☐   ☐   ☐   Adams, Cleve F.
                    Sabotage *or Death Before
                    Breakfast;* or *Death at
                    the Dam* (1940)
☐   ☐   ☐   The Private Eye (1942)

☐   ☐   ☐   Adams, Samuel Hopkins
                    Average Jones (1911)

☐   ☐   ☐   Allen, Grant
                    An African Millionaire
                    (1897)

                  Allingham, Margery
☐   ☐   ☐   Death of a Ghost (1934)
☐   ☐   ☐   Flowers for the Judge *or
                    Legacy in Blood* (1936)
☐   ☐   ☐   Dancers in Mourning *or Who
                    Killed Chloe?* (1937)
☐   ☐   ☐   The Case of the Late Pig
                    (1937)
☐   ☐   ☐   The Fashion in Shrouds
                    (1938)
☐   ☐   ☐   Mr. Campion and Others
                    (1939)

                  Ambler, Eric
☐   ☐   ☐   The Dark Frontier (1936)
☐   ☐   ☐   A Coffin for Dimitrios *or
                    The Mask of Dimitrios*
                    (1939)
☐   ☐   ☐   Journey Into Fear (1940)

```
Books I:
Have
Read   Want   Own
                      Anderson, Frederick Irving
 []     []     []       The Notorious Sophie Lang
                          (1925)
 []     []     []       The Book of Murder (1930)

                      Antheil, George
 []     []     []       Death in the Dark (1930)

                      Armstrong, Charlotte
 []     []     []       The Unsuspected (1946)

                      Ashby, R.C.
 []     []     []       Death on Tiptoe (1930)
 []     []     []       He Arrived at Dusk (1933)

                      Ashdown, Clifford
 []     []     []       The Adventures of Romney
                          Pringle (1902)

                      Other Books/Notes:

 []     []     []     _____
 []     []     []     _____
 []     []     []     _____
 []     []     []     _____
 []     []     []     _____
 []     []     []     _____
```

Books I:
Have
Read   Want   Own

                        Bailey, H.C.
☐   ☐   ☐   Call Mr. Fortune (1920)
☐   ☐   ☐   The Red Castle Mystery
                                (1932)
☐   ☐   ☐   The Bishop's Crime (1940)
                                [included in *Meet Mr.
                                Fortune*]
☐   ☐   ☐   Orphan Ann *or The Little
                                Captain* (1941)
☐   ☐   ☐   Meet Mr. Fortune (1942)

                        Balmer, Edwin and
                        MacHarg, William
☐   ☐   ☐   The Achievements of Luther
                                Trant (1910)

                        Balzac, Honore de
☐   ☐   ☐   Histoire des Treize (1835)
☐   ☐   ☐   Pere Goriot (1835)

                        Bardin, John Franklin
☐   ☐   ☐   The Deadly Percheron (1946)
☐   ☐   ☐   The Last of Philip Banter
                                (1947)
☐   ☐   ☐   Devil Take the Blue-Tail
                                Fly (1948)

                        Barr, Robert
☐   ☐   ☐   The Triumphs of Eugene
                                Valmont (1906)

Books I:
Have
Read Want Own

☐   ☐   ☐   Beeding, Francis
                    The House of Dr. Edwardes
                      or *Spellbound* (1927)
☐   ☐   ☐   Death Walks in Eastrepps
                      (1931)

                  Bell, Josephine
☐   ☐   ☐   Murder in Hospital (1937)
☐   ☐   ☐   Curtain Call for a Corpse
                      or *Death at Half-Term*
                      (1939)
☐   ☐   ☐   From Natural Causes (1939)
☐   ☐   ☐   Death at the Medical Board
                      (1944)

                  Bellairs, George
☐   ☐   ☐   Death of a Busybody (1934)

                  Bennett, Arnold
☐   ☐   ☐   The Grand Babylon Hotel
                      (1902)
☐   ☐   ☐   The Loot of Cities (1905)

                  Bennett, Margot
☐   ☐   ☐   Time to Change Hats (1945)

                  Benson, Godfrey R.
☐   ☐   ☐   Tracks in the Snow (1906)

Books I:
Have
Read Want Own

☐   ☐   ☐   Bentley, E.C.
                    Trent's Last Case or The
                      Woman in Black (1913)
☐   ☐   ☐   Trent's Own Case (1936)
☐   ☐   ☐   Trent Intervenes (1938)

                  Berkeley, Anthony
☐   ☐   ☐   The Wychford Poisoning Case
                    (1926)
☐   ☐   ☐   The Poisoned Chocolates
                    Case (1929)
☐   ☐   ☐   The Piccadilly Murder
                    (1929)
☐   ☐   ☐   Trial and Error (1937)

                  Bierstadt, Edward
☐   ☐   ☐   Satan Was a Man (1935)

                  Biggers, Earl Derr
☐   ☐   ☐   The House Without a Key
                    (1925)
☐   ☐   ☐   The Chinese Parrot (1926)

                  Blake, Nicholas
☐   ☐   ☐   The Beast Must Die (1938)
☐   ☐   ☐   The Case of the Abominable
                    Snowman or The Corpse in
                    the Snowman (1941)
☐   ☐   ☐   Minute for Murder (1947)

                  Bodkin, M. McDonnell
☐   ☐   ☐   Paul Beck, The Rule of
                    Thumb Detective (1898)

Books I:
Have
Read   Want   Own

☐   ☐   ☐   Bosworth, Allan
                      Full Crash Dive (1942)

☐   ☐   ☐   Borges, Jorge Luis and
                    Bioy-Casares, Adolfo
                      Six Problems for Don Isidro
                      Parodi (1942) [originally
                      by "H. Bustos Domecq"]

                    Boucher, Anthony
☐   ☐   ☐   The Case of the Seven
                      of Calvary (1937)
☐   ☐   ☐   The Case of the Crumpled
                      Knave (1939)
☐   ☐   ☐   The Case of the Baker
                      Street Irregulars or
                      Blood on Baker Street
                      (1940)

                    Boutell, Anita
☐   ☐   ☐   Death Has a Past (1939)

                    Bowers, Dorothy
☐   ☐   ☐   Fear and Miss Betony (1942)
☐   ☐   ☐   The Bells at Old Bailey
                      (1947)

                    Braddon, Mary Elizabeth
☐   ☐   ☐   Lady Audley's Secret (1862)

                    Brahms, Caryl and Simon, S.J.
☐   ☐   ☐   A Bullet in the Ballet
                      (1937)

Books I:
 Have
 Read Want Own

☐ ☐ ☐ Bramah, Ernest
         Max Carrados (1914)

         Brand, Christianna
☐ ☐ ☐   Heads You Lose (1941)
☐ ☐ ☐   Green for Danger (1944)
☐ ☐ ☐   Cat and Mouse (1950)

         Branson, H.C.
☐ ☐ ☐   I'll Eat You Last or I'll
           Kill You Last (1941)
☐ ☐ ☐   The Pricking Thumb (1943)
☐ ☐ ☐   The Case of the Giant
           Killer (1944)

         Brean, Herbert
☐ ☐ ☐   Wilders Walk Away (1948)

         Brock, Lynn
☐ ☐ ☐   Colonel Gore's Third Case:
           The Kink (1925)
☐ ☐ ☐   The Stoat (1940)

         Brown, Frederic
☐ ☐ ☐   The Fabulous Clipjoint
           (1947)

         Buchan, John
☐ ☐ ☐   The Thirty-Nine Steps
           (1915)

         Bullett, Gerald
☐ ☐ ☐   The Jury (1935)
☐ ☐ ☐   Judgment in Suspense (1946)

- 11 -

Books I:
Have
Read   Want   Own:

                        Bulwer-Lytton
☐   ☐   ☐   Pelham (1828)
☐   ☐   ☐   Eugene Aram (1832)

                        Burgess, Gelett
☐   ☐   ☐   The Master of Mysteries
                            (1912)
☐   ☐   ☐   Ladies in Boxes (1942)

                        Burke, Thomas
☐   ☐   ☐   Limehouse Nights: Tales of
                            Chinatown (1916)

                        Burnett, W.R.
☐   ☐   ☐   Little Caesar (1929)
☐   ☐   ☐   The Asphalt Jungle (1949)

                        Butler, Ellis Parker
☐   ☐   ☐   Philo Gubb: Correspondence
                            School Detective (1918)

                        Other Books/Notes:

☐   ☐   ☐   _____

☐   ☐   ☐   _____

☐   ☐   ☐   _____

☐   ☐   ☐   _____

☐   ☐   ☐   _____

Books I:
Have
Read Want Own

☐ ☐ ☐ Cadett, Herbert
          The Adventures of a
            Journalist (1900)

          Cain, James M.
☐ ☐ ☐   The Postman Always Rings
              Twice (1934)
☐ ☐ ☐   Double Indemnity (1944)

          Cannan, Joanna
☐ ☐ ☐   Death at "The Dog" (1940)
☐ ☐ ☐   Poisonous Relations or
              The Taste of Murder; or
              Murder Included (1950)

          Capes, Bernard
☐ ☐ ☐   The Skeleton Key (1919)

          Carleton, Marjorie
☐ ☐ ☐   The Bride Regrets (1950)

          Carpenter, Margaret
☐ ☐ ☐   Experiment Perilous (1943)

          Carr, John Dickson
☐ ☐ ☐   The Three Coffins or The
              Hollow Man (1935)
☐ ☐ ☐   The Burning Court (1937)
☐ ☐ ☐   The Crooked Hinge (1938)
☐ ☐ ☐   The Bride of Newgate (1950)

          Carter, Nicholas
☐ ☐ ☐   The Detective's Pretty
              Neighbor (1899)

Books I:
Have
Read Want Own

☐   ☐   ☐   Caspary, Vera
                  Laura (1943)

                Chandler, Raymond
☐   ☐   ☐   The Big Sleep (1939)
☐   ☐   ☐   Farewell, My Lovely (1940)
☐   ☐   ☐   The High Window (1942)
☐   ☐   ☐   The Lady in the Lake (1943)
☐   ☐   ☐   Five Murderers (1944)

                Charteris, Leslie
☐   ☐   ☐   The Brighter Buccaneer
                    (1933)
☐   ☐   ☐   The Saint in New York
                    (1935)

                Chase, James Hadley
☐   ☐   ☐   No Orchids for Miss
                    Blandish or The Villain
                    and the Virgin (1939)

                Chester, George Randolph
☐   ☐   ☐   Get-Rich-Quick Wallingford
                    (1908)

                Chesterton, G.K.
☐   ☐   ☐   The Man Who Was Thursday:
                    A Nightmare (1908)
☐   ☐   ☐   The Innocence of Father
                    Brown (1911)

Books I:
Have
Read Want Own

                         Cheyney, Peter
☐   ☐   ☐   This Man Is Dangerous (1936)
☐   ☐   ☐   Dark Duet *or The Counter Spy Murders* (1942)

                         Childers, Erskine
☐   ☐   ☐   The Riddle of the Sands (1903)

                         Christie, Agatha
☐   ☐   ☐   The Mysterious Affair at Styles (1920)
☐   ☐   ☐   Poirot Investigates (1924)
☐   ☐   ☐   The Murder of Roger Ackroyd (1926)
☐   ☐   ☐   The Murder at the Vicarage (1930)
☐   ☐   ☐   The ABC Murders *or The Alphabet Murders* (1936)
☐   ☐   ☐   Murder in Retrospect *or Five Little Pigs* (1942)
☐   ☐   ☐   Witness for the Prosecution (1948)

                         Clason, Clyde B.
☐   ☐   ☐   The Man from Tibet (1938)

                         Clements, E.H.
☐   ☐   ☐   Let Him Die (1939)
☐   ☐   ☐   Perhaps a Little Danger (1942)

Books I:
Have
Read Want Own

☐ ☐ ☐ Clouston, J. Storer
            Carrington's Cases (1920)

☐ ☐ ☐ Cobb, Irvin S.
            Faith, Hope and Charity
            (1934)

☐ ☐ ☐ Cohen, Octavus Roy
            Jim Hanvey, Detective
            (1923)

☐ ☐ ☐ Cole, G.D.H.
            The Brooklyn Murders (1923)

         Cole, G.D.H. and Margaret
☐ ☐ ☐   Superintendent Wilson's
            Holiday (1928)
☐ ☐ ☐   Death in the Quarry (1934)

         Coles, Manning
☐ ☐ ☐   Drink to Yesterday (1940)
☐ ☐ ☐   A Toast to Tomorrow or
            Pray Silence (1940)

         Collins, Wilkie
☐ ☐ ☐   The Woman in White (1860)
☐ ☐ ☐   Armadale (1866)
☐ ☐ ☐   The Moonstone (1868)

         Connell, Richard
☐ ☐ ☐   "The Most Dangerous Game"
            (1925)

Books I:
Have
Read Want Own

☐ ☐ ☐ Connington, J.J.
           The Eye in the Museum
              (1929)
☐ ☐ ☐   The Sweepstake Murders
              (1931)

           Conrad, Joseph
☐ ☐ ☐   The Secret Agent (1907)

           Cores, Lucy
☐ ☐ ☐   Painted for the Kill (1943)

           Coxe, George Harmon
☐ ☐ ☐   Murder with Pictures (1935)

           Cozzens, James Gould
☐ ☐ ☐   The Just and the Unjust
              (1942)

           Crane, Frances
☐ ☐ ☐   The Turquoise Shop (1941)

           Crispin, Edmund
☐ ☐ ☐   The Moving Toyshop (1946)
☐ ☐ ☐   Love Lies Bleeding (1948)

           Crofts, Freeman Wills
☐ ☐ ☐   The Cask (1920)
☐ ☐ ☐   Inspector French's Greatest
              Case (1925)
☐ ☐ ☐   The 12:30 from Croydon *or*
              Wilful and Premeditated
              (1934)

Books I:
Have
Read   Want   Own

☐   ☐   ☐   Cunningham, A.B.
                         The Strange Death of
                            Manny Square (1941)

                     Other Books/Notes:

☐   ☐   ☐   _____
☐   ☐   ☐   _____
☐   ☐   ☐   _____
☐   ☐   ☐   _____
☐   ☐   ☐   _____
☐   ☐   ☐   _____
☐   ☐   ☐   _____
☐   ☐   ☐   _____
☐   ☐   ☐   _____
☐   ☐   ☐   _____
☐   ☐   ☐   _____
☐   ☐   ☐   _____
☐   ☐   ☐   _____

Books I:
 Have
 Read Want Own

☐ ☐ ☐ Daly, Carroll John
            The Snarl of the Beast
              (1927)
☐ ☐ ☐   Emperor of Evil (1936)

         Daly, Elizabeth
☐ ☐ ☐   Unexpected Night (1940)
☐ ☐ ☐   Murders in Volume 2 (1941)
☐ ☐ ☐   The House Without the Door
              (1942)
☐ ☐ ☐   Arrow Pointing Nowhere or
              Murder Listens In (1944)

         Dane, Clemence and
         Simpson, Helen
☐ ☐ ☐   Enter Sir John (1928)
☐ ☐ ☐   Re-enter Sir John (1932)

         Davis, Mildred
☐ ☐ ☐   The Room Upstairs (1948)

         Davis, Richard Harding
☐ ☐ ☐   In the Fog (1901)

         Dean, Elizabeth
☐ ☐ ☐   Murder Is a Collector's
              Item (1939)

         Dean, Robert George
☐ ☐ ☐   Murder by Marriage (1940)

Books I:
Have
Read   Want   Own

☐   ☐   ☐   De la Torre, Lillian
☐   ☐   ☐   Elizabeth Is Missing (1945)
                            Dr. Sam: Johnson, Detector
                                (1946)

                        Dickens, Charles
☐   ☐   ☐   Bleak House (1853)
☐   ☐   ☐   The Mystery of Edwin Drood
                                (1870) *[unfinished]*

                        Dickson, Carter
                        (John Dickson Carr)
☐   ☐   ☐   The Red Widow Murders
                                (1935)
☐   ☐   ☐   The Judas Window *or The
                                Crossbow Murder* (1938)
☐   ☐   ☐   The Department of Queer
                                Complaints (1940)
☐   ☐   ☐   The Curse of the Bronze
                                Lamp *or Lord of the
                                Sorcerers* (1945)

                        Dodge, David
☐   ☐   ☐   Death and Taxes (1941)

                        Donovan, Dick
☐   ☐   ☐   The Man-Hunter: Stories
                                from the Note-Book of
                                a Detective (1888)

                        Dostoevsky, Feodor
☐   ☐   ☐   Crime and Punishment (1866)

Books I:
Have
Read Want Own

☐ ☐ ☐ **Dougal, Lily**
             The Summit House Mystery
             (1905)

             Doyle, Sir Arthur Conan
☐ ☐ ☐   A Study in Scarlet (1888)
☐ ☐ ☐   The Sign of Four (1890)
☐ ☐ ☐   The Adventures of Sherlock
                Holmes (1892)
☐ ☐ ☐   The Memoirs of Sherlock
                Holmes (1894)
☐ ☐ ☐   The Hound of the
                Baskervilles (1902)
☐ ☐ ☐   The Return of Sherlock
                Holmes (1905)
☐ ☐ ☐   The Valley of Fear (1914)
☐ ☐ ☐   His Last Bow: Some
                Reminiscences of Sherlock
                Holmes (1917)
☐ ☐ ☐   The Case-Book of Sherlock
                Holmes (1927)

             Dreiser, Theodore
☐ ☐ ☐   An American Tragedy (1925)

             Du Bois, Theodora
☐ ☐ ☐   Death Wears a White Coat
                (1938)

             Duke, Winifred
☐ ☐ ☐   The Laird (1925)
☐ ☐ ☐   Skin for Skin (1935)
☐ ☐ ☐   Crookedshaws (1936)

Books I:
Have
Read   Want   Own

☐   ☐   ☐   Du Maurier, Daphne
                            Rebecca (1938)

                        Other Books/Notes:

☐   ☐   ☐   _____

☐   ☐   ☐   _____

☐   ☐   ☐   _____

☐   ☐   ☐   _____

☐   ☐   ☐   _____

☐   ☐   ☐   _____

☐   ☐   ☐   _____

☐   ☐   ☐   _____

☐   ☐   ☐   _____

☐   ☐   ☐   _____

☐   ☐   ☐   _____

☐   ☐   ☐   _____

☐   ☐   ☐   _____

☐   ☐   ☐   _____

Books I:
Have
Read Want Own

☐ ☐ ☐ Eberhart, Mignon C.
☐ ☐ ☐   The Patient in Room 18 (1929)
☐ ☐ ☐   While the Patient Slept (1930)
☐ ☐ ☐   The Cases of Susan Dare (1934)
          Fair Warning (1936)

☐ ☐ ☐ Eustis, Helen
            The Horizontal Man (1946)

Other Books/Notes:

☐ ☐ ☐ _____

☐ ☐ ☐ _____

☐ ☐ ☐ _____

☐ ☐ ☐ _____

☐ ☐ ☐ _____

☐ ☐ ☐ _____

☐ ☐ ☐ _____

☐ ☐ ☐ _____

☐ ☐ ☐ _____

Books I:
Have
Read Want Own

  ☐   ☐   ☐   Fair, A.A.
                  (Erle Stanley Gardner)
                  The Bigger They Come (1939)

  ☐   ☐   ☐   Falkner, John Meade
                  The Nebuly Coat (1903)

  ☐   ☐   ☐   Fast, Julius
                  Watchful at Night (1945)

                  Faulkner, William
  ☐   ☐   ☐   Intruder in the Dust
                    (1948)
  ☐   ☐   ☐   Knight's Gambit (1949)

                  Fearing, Kenneth
  ☐   ☐   ☐   The Big Clock (1946)

                  Fitt, Mary
  ☐   ☐   ☐   Death and the Pleasant
                    Voices (1946)

                  Fletcher, J.S.
  ☐   ☐   ☐   The Adventures of Archer
                    Dawe, Sleuth-Hound *or*
                    The Contents of the
                    Coffin (1909)
  ☐   ☐   ☐   The Middle Temple Murder
                    (1918)
  ☐   ☐   ☐   The Charing Cross Mystery
                    (1923)

Books I:
Have
Read Want Own

☐   ☐   ☐   Fletcher, Lucille
                    Sorry, Wrong Number (1944)

☐   ☐   ☐   Forbes, Esther
                    The General's Lady (1938)

                 Ford, Leslie
☐   ☐   ☐   The Simple Way of Poison
                      (1937)
☐   ☐   ☐   Ill Met By Moonlight (1937)
☐   ☐   ☐   Three Bright Pebbles (1938)

                 Forester, C.S.
☐   ☐   ☐   Payment Deferred (1926)
☐   ☐   ☐   Plain Murder (1930)

                 Freeman, R. Austin
☐   ☐   ☐   The Red Thumb Mark (1907)
☐   ☐   ☐   John Thorndyke's Cases or
                      Dr. Thorndyke's Cases
                      (1909)
☐   ☐   ☐   The Eye of Osiris: A
                      Detective Romance or The
                      Vanishing Man (1911)
☐   ☐   ☐   The Singing Bone or The
                      Adventures of Dr.
                      Thorndyke (1912)
☐   ☐   ☐   The Mystery of Angelina
                      Frood (1924)
☐   ☐   ☐   Mr. Pottermack's Oversight
                      (1930)

- 25 -

Books I:
Have
Read Want Own

☐ ☐ ☐ Frome, David
☐ ☐ ☐   The Hammersmith Murders (1930)
☐ ☐ ☐   The Man from Scotland Yard or Mr. Simpson Finds a Body (1932)

☐ ☐ ☐ Fuller, Timothy
☐ ☐ ☐   Harvard Has a Homicide (1936)
☐ ☐ ☐   Reunion with Murder (1941)

☐ ☐ ☐ Futrelle, Jacques
  The Thinking Machine or The Problem of Cell 13 (1907)

Other Books/Notes:

☐ ☐ ☐ _____
☐ ☐ ☐ _____
☐ ☐ ☐ _____
☐ ☐ ☐ _____
☐ ☐ ☐ _____
☐ ☐ ☐ _____
☐ ☐ ☐ _____

Books I:
Have
Read Want Own

          Gaboriau, Emile
☐   ☐   ☐   The Mystery of Orcival *or*
                  Crime at Orcival (1871)
☐   ☐   ☐   The Widow Lerouge *or The*
                  Lerouge Case (1873)
☐   ☐   ☐   Monsieur Lecoq (1880)
☐   ☐   ☐   The Little Old Man of the
                  Batignolles (1880)
☐   ☐   ☐   File No. 113 *or Warrant No.*
                  113; or The Blackmailer
                  (1883)

          Gardner, Erle Stanley
☐   ☐   ☐   The Case of the Velvet
                  Claws (1933)
☐   ☐   ☐   The Case of the Sulky Girl
                  (1933)
☐   ☐   ☐   The Case of the Counterfeit
                  Eye (1935)

          Gilbert, Anthony
☐   ☐   ☐   Mystery in the Woodshed
                  or Something Nasty in the
                  Woodshed (1942)

          Gilbert, Michael
☐   ☐   ☐   Smallbone Deceased (1950)

          Gillette, William
☐   ☐   ☐   The Astounding Crime in
                  Torrington Road (1927)

          Glaspell, Susan
☐   ☐   ☐   A Jury of Her Peers (1927)

Books I:
Have
Read Want Own

☐   ☐   ☐   Godwin, William
              Things As They Are; or The
                Adventures of Caleb
                Williams (1794)

☐   ☐   ☐   Goodchild, George and
              Roberts, Bechhofer
                The Dear Old Gentleman
                (1935)

☐   ☐   ☐   Green, Alan
                What A Body! (1949)

☐   ☐   ☐   Greene, Anna Katharine
                The Leavenworth Case: A
                Lawyer's Story (1878)
☐   ☐   ☐   Masterpieces of Mystery or
                Room Number 3 and Other
                Stories (1913)

☐   ☐   ☐   Greene, Graham
                This Gun for Hire or A Gun
                for Sale (1936)
☐   ☐   ☐   Brighton Rock (1938)
☐   ☐   ☐   The Confidential Agent
                (1939)
☐   ☐   ☐   The Third Man (1950)

☐   ☐   ☐   Greene, Ward
                Death in the Deep South
                (1936)

☐   ☐   ☐   Grey, A.F.
                Momentary Stoppage (1942)

Books I:
Have
Read　Want　Own

☐　☐　☐　Groller, Balduin
　　　　　　　Detective Dagobert's Deeds
　　　　　　　　and Adventures (1908)

☐　☐　☐　Gruber, Frank
　　　　　　　The French Key *or Once
　　　　　　　　Over Deadly* (1940)
☐　☐　☐　　Kiss the Boss Goodbye *or
　　　　　　　　The Last Doorbell* (1941)
　　　　　　　[as John K. Vedder]

　　　　　　Other Books/Notes:

☐　☐　☐　_____
☐　☐　☐　_____
☐　☐　☐　_____
☐　☐　☐　_____
☐　☐　☐　_____
☐　☐　☐　_____
☐　☐　☐　_____
☐　☐　☐　_____
☐　☐　☐　_____
☐　☐　☐　_____

Books I:
Have
Read Want Own

☐ ☐ ☐ Halliday, Brett
    Murder Is My Business (1945)

☐ ☐ ☐ Halsey, Harlan Page
    Old Sleuth, the Detective (1885)

Hamilton, Bruce
☐ ☐ ☐   To Be Hanged (1930)
☐ ☐ ☐   Dead Reckoning or Middle Class Murder (1937)

Hamilton, Patrick
☐ ☐ ☐   Rope or Rope's End (1929)
☐ ☐ ☐   Angel Street or Gaslight (1938)
☐ ☐ ☐   Hangover Square; or, The Man with Two Minds (1941)

Hammett, Dashiell
☐ ☐ ☐   The Maltese Falcon (1930)
☐ ☐ ☐   The Glass Key (1931)
☐ ☐ ☐   The Thin Man (1934)
☐ ☐ ☐   The Adventures of Sam Spade and Other Stories or They Can Only Hang You Once; or A Man Called Spade (1944)
☐ ☐ ☐   The Continental Op (1945)
☐ ☐ ☐   The Return of the Continental Op (1945)

Books I:
Have
Read Want Own

☐   ☐   ☐   Hanshew, Thomas W.
                 The Man of the Forty Faces
                 (1910)
☐   ☐   ☐   Cleek of Scotland Yard
                 (1914)

☐   ☐   ☐   Hardy, Arthur Sherburne
                 Diane and Her Friends
                 (1914)
☐   ☐   ☐   No. 13, Rue du Bon Diable
                 (1917)

                Hare, Cyril
☐   ☐   ☐   Tenant for Death (1937)
☐   ☐   ☐   Tragedy at Law (1942)

                Hart, Frances Noyes
☐   ☐   ☐   The Bellamy Trial (1927)

                Harte, Bret
☐   ☐   ☐   Condensed Novels (1902)

                Head, Matthew
☐   ☐   ☐   The Smell of Money (1943)
☐   ☐   ☐   The Cabinda Affair (1949)

                Heard, H.F.
☐   ☐   ☐   A Taste for Honey or A
                 Taste for Murder (1941)
☐   ☐   ☐   Reply Paid (1942)

                Helu, Antonio
☐   ☐   ☐   The Compulsion to Murder
                 (1946)

Books I:
Have
Read Want Own

			Heyer, Georgette
☐	☐	☐	Merely Murder (1935)
☐	☐	☐	A Blunt Instrument (1938)
☐	☐	☐	Envious Casca (1941)

Highsmith, Patricia
☐ ☐ ☐ Strangers on a Train (1950)

Hilliard, A.R.
☐ ☐ ☐ Justice Be Damned (1941)

Hilton, James (Glen Trevor)
☐ ☐ ☐ Was It Murder? or *Murder at School* (1933)

Hocking, Anne
☐ ☐ ☐ Deadly Is the Evil Tongue or *Old Mrs. Fitzgerald* (1939)
☐ ☐ ☐ Prussian Blue or *The Finishing Touch* (1947)

Hodgson, William Hope
☐ ☐ ☐ *Carnacki, the Ghost Finder* (1913)

Holding, Elizabeth Sanxay
☐ ☐ ☐ The Obstinate Murderer or *No Harm Intended* (1938)
☐ ☐ ☐ Lady Killer (1942)

Books I:
Have
Read Want Own

☐ ☐ ☐ Holmes, H.H.
            (Anthony Boucher)
              Rocket to the Morgue (1942)

☐ ☐ ☐ Homes, Geoffrey
              The Doctor Died at Dusk
                (1936)

☐ ☐ ☐ Hornung, E.W.
              The Amateur Cracksman *or*
                Raffles, The Amateur
                Cracksman (1899)
☐ ☐ ☐   A Thief in the Night (1905)

☐ ☐ ☐ Household, Geoffrey
              Rogue Male *or Man Hunt*
                (1939)

          Hughes, Dorothy B.
☐ ☐ ☐   The So Blue Marble (1940)
☐ ☐ ☐   The Fallen Sparrow (1942)
☐ ☐ ☐   The Delicate Ape (1944)
☐ ☐ ☐   In a Lonely Place (1947)

☐ ☐ ☐ Hugo, Victor
              Les Miserables (1862)

☐ ☐ ☐ Hull, Richard
              The Murder of My Aunt
                (1934)

☐ ☐ ☐ Hume, Fergus W.
              The Mystery of a Hansom
                Cab (1886)

- 33 -

Books I:
Have
Read   Want   Own

☐   ☐   ☐   Huxley, Elspeth
                     Murder at Government House (1937)
☐   ☐   ☐   Murder on Safari (1938)

                   Other Books/Notes:

☐   ☐   ☐   _____
☐   ☐   ☐   _____
☐   ☐   ☐   _____
☐   ☐   ☐   _____
☐   ☐   ☐   _____
☐   ☐   ☐   _____
☐   ☐   ☐   _____
☐   ☐   ☐   _____
☐   ☐   ☐   _____
☐   ☐   ☐   _____
☐   ☐   ☐   _____
☐   ☐   ☐   _____
☐   ☐   ☐   _____

Books I:
Have
Read　Want　Own

　　　　　　　　　　Iles, Francis
　　　　　　　　　　(Anthony Berkeley)
☐　　☐　　☐　　　Malice Aforethought (1931)
☐　　☐　　☐　　　Before the Fact (1932)
☐　　☐　　☐　　　As for the Woman (1939)

　　　　　　　　　　Innes, Michael
☐　　☐　　☐　　　Death at the President's
　　　　　　　　　　　Lodging *or Seven*
　　　　　　　　　　　Suspects (1936)
☐　　☐　　☐　　　Hamlet, Revenge! (1937)
☐　　☐　　☐　　　Lament for a Maker (1938)

　　　　　　　　　　Irish, William
　　　　　　　　　　(Cornell Woolrich)
☐　　☐　　☐　　　Phantom Lady (1942)
☐　　☐　　☐　　　After-Dinner Story *or Six*
　　　　　　　　　　　Times Death (1944)
☐　　☐　　☐　　　Waltz into Darkness (1947)

　　　　　　　　　　Other Books/Notes:

☐　　☐　　☐　　　_____
☐　　☐　　☐　　　_____
☐　　☐　　☐　　　_____
☐　　☐　　☐　　　_____
☐　　☐　　☐　　　_____
☐　　☐　　☐　　　_____

Books I:
Have
Read   Want   Own

☐   ☐   ☐   James, Henry
☐   ☐   ☐   The Other House (1896)
                      The Turn of the Screw
                        (1898)

                    Jarrett, Cora
☐   ☐   ☐   Night over Fitch's Pond
                        (1933)

                    Jepson, Selwyn
☐   ☐   ☐   Keep Murder Quiet (1940)
☐   ☐   ☐   Man Running or Outrun the
                        Constable; or Killer by
                        Proxy (1948)

                    Jesse, F. Tennyson
☐   ☐   ☐   The Solange Stories (1931)
☐   ☐   ☐   A Pin to See the Peepshow
                        (1934)

                    Johns, Veronica Parker
☐   ☐   ☐   The Singing Widow (1941)

                    Johnson, W. Bolingbroke
☐   ☐   ☐   The Widening Stain (1942)

                    Other Books/Notes:

☐   ☐   ☐   _____

☐   ☐   ☐   _____

☐   ☐   ☐   _____

Books I:
 Have
 Read Want Own

                       Keene, Faraday
☐   ☐   ☐   Pattern in Black and Red (1934)

                       Keith, David
☐   ☐   ☐   A Matter of Iodine (1940)

                       Kendrick, Baynard H.
☐   ☐   ☐   The Odor of Violets *or* Eyes in the Night (1941)
☐   ☐   ☐   Death Knell (1945)

                       Keverne, Richard
☐   ☐   ☐   The Man in the Red Hat (1930)

                       King, C. Daly
☐   ☐   ☐   The Curious Mr. Tarrant (1935)
☐   ☐   ☐   Obelists Fly High (1935)

                       King, Rufus
☐   ☐   ☐   Murder by the Clock (1929)
☐   ☐   ☐   Valcour Meets Murder (1932)
☐   ☐   ☐   Profile of a Murder (1935)

                       Kitchin, C.H.B.
☐   ☐   ☐   Death of My Aunt (1929)

                       Knox, Ronald A.
☐   ☐   ☐   The Viaduct Murder (1925)

Books I:
Have
Read Want Own

☐　　☐　　☐　　Kutak, Rosemary
　　　　　　　　　　Darkness of Slumber (1944)

　　　　　　　　Other Books/Notes:

☐　　☐　　☐　　_____
☐　　☐　　☐　　_____
☐　　☐　　☐　　_____
☐　　☐　　☐　　_____
☐　　☐　　☐　　_____
☐　　☐　　☐　　_____
☐　　☐　　☐　　_____
☐　　☐　　☐　　_____
☐　　☐　　☐　　_____
☐　　☐　　☐　　_____
☐　　☐　　☐　　_____
☐　　☐　　☐　　_____
☐　　☐　　☐　　_____
☐　　☐　　☐　　_____

Books I:
Have
Read Want Own

☐ ☐ ☐ Latimer, Jonathan
           Headed for a Hearse or
              The Westland Case (1935)
☐ ☐ ☐   The Lady in the Morgue
              (1936)

           Lawrence, Hilda
☐ ☐ ☐   Blood upon the Snow (1944)
☐ ☐ ☐   A Time to Die (1945)
☐ ☐ ☐   Death of a Doll (1947)

           Leblanc, Maurice
☐ ☐ ☐   Arsene Lupin, Gentleman-
              Cambrioleur (1907)
☐ ☐ ☐   813 (1910)
☐ ☐ ☐   The Crystal Stopper (1913)
☐ ☐ ☐   The Teeth of the Tiger
              (1914)
☐ ☐ ☐   The Eight Strokes of the
              Clock (1922)

           Lees, Hannah and Bachmann,
           Lawrence
☐ ☐ ☐   Death in the Doll's House
              (1943)

           Le Fanu, Joseph Sheridan
☐ ☐ ☐   Uncle Silas (1864)
☐ ☐ ☐   Wylder's Hand (1864)

           Le Queux, William
☐ ☐ ☐   Mysteries of the Great
              City (1919)

Books I:
Have
Read Want Own

☐ ☐ ☐ Leroux, Gaston
　　　　　The Mystery of the Yellow Room *or Murder in the Bedroom* (1908)
☐ ☐ ☐ 　The Phantom of the Opera (1911)

☐ ☐ ☐ Lewis, Alfred Henry
　　　　　Confessions of a Detective (1906)

☐ ☐ ☐ Lewis, Lange
☐ ☐ ☐ 　Meat for Murder (1943)
　　　　　The Birthday Murder (1945)

　　　　Lockridge, Frances and Richard
☐ ☐ ☐ 　The Norths Meet Murder (1940)
☐ ☐ ☐ 　Murder Out of Turn (1941)

☐ ☐ ☐ Lombard, Nap
☐ ☐ ☐ 　Tidy Death (1940)
　　　　　Murder's a Swine (1942)

☐ ☐ ☐ Lorac, E.C.R.
　　　　　Murder in St. John's Wood (1934)
☐ ☐ ☐ 　Death of an Author (1935)
☐ ☐ ☐ 　Murder by Matchlight (1945)

Books I:
Have
Read Want Own

☐ ☐ ☐ Lowndes, Mrs. Belloc
☐ ☐ ☐   The Lodger (1913)
☐ ☐ ☐   What Really Happened (1926)
☐ ☐ ☐   Letty Lynton (1931)
           Lizzie Borden: A Study in
             Conjecture (1939)

         Luhrs, Victor
☐ ☐ ☐   The Longbow Murder (1941)

         Lustgarten, Edgar
☐ ☐ ☐   One More Unfortunate or A
             Case to Answer (1947)

         Lyell, William Darling
☐ ☐ ☐   The House in Queen Anne's
             Square (1920)

         Other Books/Notes:

☐ ☐ ☐   _____
☐ ☐ ☐   _____
☐ ☐ ☐   _____
☐ ☐ ☐   _____
☐ ☐ ☐   _____
☐ ☐ ☐   _____

Books I:
Have
Read Want Own

☐ ☐ ☐
☐ ☐ ☐
☐ ☐ ☐

MacDonald, Philip
   The Rasp (1924)
   Murder Gone Mad (1931)
   Warrant for X or The
   Nursemaid Who
   Disappeared (1938)

☐ ☐ ☐
☐ ☐ ☐

Macdonald, Ross
   The Moving Target (1949)
   The Drowning Pool (1950)

☐ ☐ ☐

MacHarg, William
   The Affairs of O'Malley
   (1940)

☐ ☐ ☐

MacInnes, Helen
   Above Suspicion (1941)

☐ ☐ ☐

Mair, John
   Never Come Back (1941)

☐ ☐ ☐

Markham, Virgil
   Death in the Dusk (1928)

☐ ☐ ☐

Marquand, John P.
   No Hero or Mr. Moto Takes a
   Hand; or your Turn, Mr.
   Moto (1935)

☐ ☐ ☐
☐ ☐ ☐
☐ ☐ ☐
☐ ☐ ☐

Marsh, Ngaio
   Death in a White Tie
   (1938)
   Overture to Death (1939)
   Colour Scheme (1943)
   Died in the Wool (1945)

Books I:
Have
Read Want Own

☐   ☐   ☐   Marsh, Richard
                    The Beetle (1915)

                  Mason, A.E.W.
☐   ☐   ☐   At the Villa Rose
                    (1910)
☐   ☐   ☐   The Four Corners of the
                    World (1917)
☐   ☐   ☐   The House of the Arrow
                    (1924)
☐   ☐   ☐   The House in Lordship Lane
                    (1946)

                  Masterman, J.C.
☐   ☐   ☐   An Oxford Tragedy
                    (1933)

                  Matthews, T.S.
☐   ☐   ☐   To the Gallows I Must Go
                    (1931)

                  Maugham, W. Somerset
☐   ☐   ☐   The Casuaring Tree *or The
                    Letter: Stories of
                    Crime* (1926)
☐   ☐   ☐   Ashenden: or, the British
                    Agent (1928)

                  McCabe, Cameron
☐   ☐   ☐   The Face on the
                    Cutting-Room Floor
                    (1937)

- 43 -

Books I:
Have
Read　Want　Own

      McCloy, Helen
☐　☐　☐ Dance of Death *or Design for Dying* (938)
☐　☐　☐ Cue for Murder (1942)
☐　☐　☐ The Goblin Market (1943)
☐　☐　☐ Through a Glass, Darkly (1950)

      McGuire, Paul
☐　☐　☐ A Funeral in Eden *or Burial Service* (1938)
☐　☐　☐ Enter Three Witches *or The Spanish Steps* (1940)

      Meade, L.T.
☐　☐　☐ Stories from the Diary of a Doctor (1894) [with Dr. Clifford Halifax]
☐　☐　☐ The Sorceress of the Strand (1903)

      M'Govan, James
☐　☐　☐ Brought to Bay (1878)

      Millar, Margaret
☐　☐　☐ The Invisible Worm (1941)
☐　☐　☐ The Devil Loves Me (1942)
☐　☐　☐ Wall of Eyes (1943)
☐　☐　☐ The Iron Gates *or Taste of Fears* (1945)

      Miller, Wade
☐　☐　☐ Deadly Weapon (1946)

Books I:
Have
Read Want Own

☐　　☐　　☐　　Millin, Sarah Gertrude
　　　　　　　　　　Three Men Die (1934)

☐　　☐　　☐　　Milne, A.A.
　　　　　　　　　　The Red House Mystery
　　　　　　　　　　　(1922)

　　　　　　　　　Mitchell, Gladys
☐　　☐　　☐　　　When Last I Died (1941)
☐　　☐　　☐　　　Laurels Are Poison (1942)
☐　　☐　　☐　　　Sunset over Soho (1943)
☐　　☐　　☐　　　The Rising of the Moon
　　　　　　　　　　　(1945)

　　　　　　　　　Moffett, Cleveland
☐　　☐　　☐　　　Through the Wall (1909)
☐　　☐　　☐　　　The Mysterious Card
　　　　　　　　　　　(1912)

　　　　　　　　　Morrison, Arthur
☐　　☐　　☐　　　Martin Hewitt,
　　　　　　　　　　　Investigator (1894)

　　　　　　　　　Muir, D.E.
☐　　☐　　☐　　　In Muffled Night (1933)

　　　　　　　　　Other Books/Notes:

☐　　☐　　☐　　_____

☐　　☐　　☐　　_____

☐　　☐　　☐　　_____

- 45 -

Books I:
Have
Read   Want   Own

☐ ☐ ☐   Norman, James
          Murder, Chop Chop (1942)

          Offord, Lenore Glen
☐ ☐ ☐   Skeleton Key (1943)
☐ ☐ ☐   The Glass Mask (1944)

          O'Flaherty, Liam
☐ ☐ ☐   The Informer (1925)

          O. Henry
☐ ☐ ☐   The Gentle Grafter
          (1908)

          O'Higgins, Harvey J.
☐ ☐ ☐   The Adventures of
          Detective Barney
          (1915)
☐ ☐ ☐   Detective Duff Unravels It
          (1929)

          Oppenheim, E. Phillips
☐ ☐ ☐   A Maker of History (1905)
☐ ☐ ☐   The Great Impersonation
          (1920)

          Orczy, Baroness
☐ ☐ ☐   The Scarlet Pimpernel
          (1905)
☐ ☐ ☐   The Old Man in the Corner
          (1909)
☐ ☐ ☐   Lady Molly of Scotland
          Yard (1910)

Books I:
Have
Read   Want   Own

☐   ☐   ☐   Ottolengui, Rodrigues
                          A Conflict of Evidence
                          (1893)
☐   ☐   ☐   Final Proof (1898)

                     Other Books/Notes:

☐   ☐   ☐   _____

☐   ☐   ☐   _____

☐   ☐   ☐   _____

☐   ☐   ☐   _____

☐   ☐   ☐   _____

☐   ☐   ☐   _____

☐   ☐   ☐   _____

☐   ☐   ☐   _____

☐   ☐   ☐   _____

☐   ☐   ☐   _____

☐   ☐   ☐   _____

☐   ☐   ☐   _____

☐   ☐   ☐   _____

Books I:
Have
Read Want Own

　　　　　　　　Page, Marco
☐　　☐　　☐　　　Fast Company (1938)
☐　　☐　　☐　　　The Shadowy Third or
　　　　　　　　　　Suspects All (1946)

　　　　　　　　Palmer, Stuart
☐　　☐　　☐　　　The Penguin Pool Murder
　　　　　　　　　　(1931)
☐　　☐　　☐　　　The Puzzle of the Blue
　　　　　　　　　　Banderilla (1937)
☐　　☐　　☐　　　The Riddles of Hildegarde
　　　　　　　　　　Withers (1947)

　　　　　　　　Patrick, Q.
　　　　　　　　(Patrick Quentin)
☐　　☐　　☐　　　S.S. Murder (1933)
☐　　☐　　☐　　　The Grindle Nightmare or
　　　　　　　　　　Darker Grows the Valley
　　　　　　　　　　(1935)

　　　　　　　　Paul, Elliott
☐　　☐　　☐　　　The Mysterious Mickey Finn
　　　　　　　　　　or Murder at the Cafe du
　　　　　　　　　　Dome (1939)

　　　　　　　　Pentecost, Hugh
☐　　☐　　☐　　　Cancelled in Red (1939)
☐　　☐　　☐　　　The 24th Horse (1940)
☐　　☐　　☐　　　The Brass Chills (1943)

　　　　　　　　Perdue, Virginia
☐　　☐　　☐　　　He Fell Down Dead (1943)
☐　　☐　　☐　　　Alarum and Excursion
　　　　　　　　　　(1944)

Books I:
Have
Read   Want   Own

☐   ☐   ☐   Phillpotts, Eden
                       My Adventure in the Flying
                           Scotsman (1888)
☐   ☐   ☐   The Grey Room (1921)
☐   ☐   ☐   The Red Redmaynes (1922)

☐   ☐   ☐   Pinkerton, Allan
                       The Expressman and the
                           Detective (1874)

☐   ☐   ☐   Player, Robert
                       The Ingenious Mr. Stone;
                           or The Documents in the
                           Langdon-Miles Case
                           (1945)

                     Poe, Edgar Allan
☐   ☐   ☐   "The Murders in the Rue
                           Morgue" (1841)
☐   ☐   ☐   "The Mystery of Marie
                           Roget" (1842)
☐   ☐   ☐   "The Gold Bug" (1843)
☐   ☐   ☐   "The Purloined Letter"
                           (1844)
☐   ☐   ☐   "Thou Art the Man" (1844)
☐   ☐   ☐   Tales (1845)

☐   ☐   ☐   Pollard, Percival
                       Lingo Dan (1903)

                     Post, Melville Davisson
☐   ☐   ☐   The Strange Schemes of
                           Randolph Mason (1896)
☐   ☐   ☐   Uncle Abner, Master of
                           Mysteries (1918)

- 49 -

Books I:
Have
Read   Want   Own

☐   ☐   ☐   Postgate, Raymond
☐   ☐   ☐   Verdict of Twelve (1940)
                          Somebody at the Door
                          (1943)

☐   ☐   ☐   Prichard, Hesketh
                          November Joe: The
                          Detective of the Woods
                          (1913)

                        Other Books/Notes:

☐   ☐   ☐   _____
☐   ☐   ☐   _____
☐   ☐   ☐   _____
☐   ☐   ☐   _____
☐   ☐   ☐   _____
☐   ☐   ☐   _____
☐   ☐   ☐   _____
☐   ☐   ☐   _____
☐   ☐   ☐   _____
☐   ☐   ☐   _____
☐   ☐   ☐   _____

Books I:
Have
Read Want Own

			Queen, Ellery
☐	☐	☐	The Roman Hat Mystery (1929)
☐	☐	☐	The Tragedy of X (1932)
☐	☐	☐	The Tragedy of Y (1932)
☐	☐	☐	The Tragedy of Z (1933)
☐	☐	☐	The Chinese Orange Mystery (1934)
☐	☐	☐	The Adventures of Ellery Queen (1934)
☐	☐	☐	Calamity Town (1942)

			Quentin, Patrick
☐	☐	☐	A Puzzle for Fools (1936)
☐	☐	☐	A Puzzle for Players (1938)

Other Books/Notes:

☐ ☐ ☐ _____

☐ ☐ ☐ _____

☐ ☐ ☐ _____

☐ ☐ ☐ _____

☐ ☐ ☐ _____

☐ ☐ ☐ _____

☐ ☐ ☐ _____

Books I:
Have
Read Want Own

☐ ☐ ☐ Rawson, Clayton
         Death from a Top Hat (1938)

☐ ☐ ☐ Raymond, Ernest
         We the Accused (1935)

☐ ☐ ☐ Reeve, Arthur B.
         The Silent Bullet: Adventures of Craig Kennedy, Scientific Detective or The Black Hand (1912)

       Rhode, John
☐ ☐ ☐   The Paddington Mystery (1925)
☐ ☐ ☐   The Murders in Praed Street (1928)
☐ ☐ ☐   Hendon's First Case (1935)
☐ ☐ ☐   The Telephone Call or Shadows of an Alibi (1946)

       Rice, Craig
☐ ☐ ☐   Trial by Fury (1941)
☐ ☐ ☐   Home Sweet Homicide (1944)

☐ ☐ ☐ Rickard, Mrs. Victor
         Not Sufficient Evidence (1926)

       Rinehart, Mary Roberts
☐ ☐ ☐   The Circular Staircase (1908)
☐ ☐ ☐   Miss Pinkerton or Double Alibi (1932)

Books I:
Have
Read   Want   Own

☐   ☐   ☐   **Robinson, B. Fletcher**
                     The Chronicles of
                       Addington Peace (1905)

☐   ☐   ☐   **Rogers, Samuel**
                     Don't Look Behind You!
                       (1944)

☐   ☐   ☐   **Rohmer, Sax**
                     The Mystery of Dr. Fu-
                       Manchu or *The Insidious
                       Dr. Fu-Manchu* (1913)
☐   ☐   ☐   The Dream-Detective (1920)

☐   ☐   ☐   **Rolls, Anthony**
                     A Clerical Error (1932)

☐   ☐   ☐   **Runyon, Damon**
                     Guys and Dolls (1931)

☐   ☐   ☐   **Russell, John**
                     The Red Mark (1919)

                     Other Books/Notes:

☐   ☐   ☐   _____

☐   ☐   ☐   _____

☐   ☐   ☐   _____

☐   ☐   ☐   _____

Books I:
Have
Read Want Own

☐ ☐ ☐   Sale, Richard
             Lazarus No. 7 or Death
                Looks In (1942)
☐ ☐ ☐   Passing Strange (1942)

           "Sapper"
           (Cyril McNeile)
☐ ☐ ☐   Bull-Dog Drummond
                (1920)

           Sayers, Dorothy L.
☐ ☐ ☐   Whose Body? (1923)
☐ ☐ ☐   The Documents in the Case
                (1930) [with Robert
                Eustace]
☐ ☐ ☐   Have His Carcase (1932)
☐ ☐ ☐   The Nine Tailors (1934)
☐ ☐ ☐   Gaudy Night (1935)

           Scherf, Margaret
☐ ☐ ☐   The Gun in Daniel
                Webster's Bust
                (1949)
☐ ☐ ☐   The Curious Custard Pie
                or Divine and Deadly
                (1950)

           Seeley, Mabel
☐ ☐ ☐   The Listening House
                (1938)

Books I:
Have
Read   Want   Own

☐   ☐   ☐   Shearing, Joseph
☐   ☐   ☐   Moss Rose (1934)
                        The Lady and the Arsenic
                        (1937)
☐   ☐   ☐   Blanch Fury or Fury's Ape
                        (1939)
☐   ☐   ☐   The Crime of Laura Sarelle
                        or Laura Sarelle (1940)
☐   ☐   ☐   Airing in a Closed
                        Carriage (1943)
☐   ☐   ☐   So Evil My Love or For
                        Her to See (1947)

                     Shelley, Mary
☐   ☐   ☐   Frankenstein (1818)

                     Shepherd, Neal
☐   ☐   ☐   Death Walks Softly (1938)

                     Shiel, M.P.
☐   ☐   ☐   Prince Zaleski (1895)

                     Simenon, Georges
☐   ☐   ☐   Maigret Stonewalled or The
                        Death of Monsieur Gallet
                        (1931)
☐   ☐   ☐   Maigret Mystified or The
                        Shadow in the Courtyard
                        (1932)
☐   ☐   ☐   Liberty Bar (1932)
☐   ☐   ☐   Maigret Goes Home (1933)
☐   ☐   ☐   Maigret and the Spinster
                        (1942)

Books I:
Have
Read Want Own

☐ ☐ ☐ Simpson, Helen
         The Prime Minister Is Dead
         (1931)

         Sims, George R.
☐ ☐ ☐   Dorcas Dene, Detective
         (1897)
☐ ☐ ☐   Clue of the Rising Moon
         (1924)
☐ ☐ ☐   Masks Off at Midnight
         (1934)

         Snow, C.P.
☐ ☐ ☐   Death Under Sail (1932)

         Spillane, Mickey
☐ ☐ ☐   I, The Jury (1947)

         Stagge, Jonathan
         (Patrick Quentin)
☐ ☐ ☐   The Stars Spell Death *or*
         Murder in the Stars
         (1939)
☐ ☐ ☐   Turn of the Table *or*
         Funeral for Five (1940)
☐ ☐ ☐   The Yellow Taxi *or* *Call a*
         Hearse (1942)

         Starrett, Vincent
☐ ☐ ☐   The Unique Hamlet (1920)
☐ ☐ ☐   Murder on "B" Deck (1929)
☐ ☐ ☐   Midnight and Percy Jones
         (1936)
☐ ☐ ☐   The Case Book of Jimmie
         Lavender (1944)

- 56 -

Books I:
Have
Read   Want   Own

                        Steel, Kurt
☐   ☐   ☐   Judas, Incorporated
                           (1939)

                        Steeves, Harrison
☐   ☐   ☐   Good Night, Sheriff
                           (1941)

                        Stevenson, Robert Louis
☐   ☐   ☐   New Arabian Nights
                           Entertainment
                           (1882)
☐   ☐   ☐   The Strange Case of Dr.
                           Jekyll and Mr. Hyde
                           (1886)

                        Stevenson, Robert Louis
                        and Osbourne, Lloyd
☐   ☐   ☐   The Wrong Box
                           (1889)
☐   ☐   ☐   The Wrecker
                           (1891)

                        Stockton, Frank R.
☐   ☐   ☐   The Lady, or the Tiger?
                           (1884)

                        Stoker, Bram
☐   ☐   ☐   Dracula (1897)

Books I:
Have
Read   Want   Own

☐ ☐ ☐ Stout, Rex
☐ ☐ ☐   Fer-de-Lance (1934)
         The League of Frightened
         Men (1935)
☐ ☐ ☐   The Rubber Band or To Kill
         Again (1936)
☐ ☐ ☐   The Red Box (1937)
☐ ☐ ☐   Too Many Cooks (1938)
☐ ☐ ☐   Some Buried Caesar or The
         Red Bull (1938)
☐ ☐ ☐   Too Many Women (1947)
☐ ☐ ☐   And Be A Villain or More
         Deaths Than One (1948)
☐ ☐ ☐   The Second Confession
         (1949)

         Strange, John Stephen
☐ ☐ ☐   Look Your Last (1943)

         Stribling, T.S.
☐ ☐ ☐   Clues of the Caribbees,
         Being Certain Criminal
         Investigations of Henry
         Poggioli, Ph.D.
         (1929)

         Strong, L.A.G.
☐ ☐ ☐   Murder Plays an Ugly Scene
         or Othello's Occupation
         (1945)

Books I:
 Have
 Read Want Own

☐ ☐ ☐   Symons, Julian
☐ ☐ ☐   The Immaterial Murder Case (1945)
☐ ☐ ☐   The Thirty-First of February (1950)

    Other Books/Notes:

☐ ☐ ☐ _____
☐ ☐ ☐ _____
☐ ☐ ☐ _____
☐ ☐ ☐ _____
☐ ☐ ☐ _____
☐ ☐ ☐ _____
☐ ☐ ☐ _____
☐ ☐ ☐ _____
☐ ☐ ☐ _____
☐ ☐ ☐ _____
☐ ☐ ☐ _____
☐ ☐ ☐ _____

Books I:
Have
Read Want Own

☐ ☐ ☐   Talbot, Hake
          Rim of the Pit (1944)

          Taylor, Phoebe Atwood
☐ ☐ ☐   The Cape Cod Mystery
          (1931)
☐ ☐ ☐   The Mystery of the Cape
          Cod Tavern (1934)

☐ ☐ ☐   Teilhet, Darwin L.
          The Talking Sparrow Murders
          (1934)

          Tey, Josephine
☐ ☐ ☐   The Man in the Queue or
          Killer in the Crowd
          (1929)
☐ ☐ ☐   Miss Pym Disposes (1946)
☐ ☐ ☐   The Franchise Affair
          (1948)
☐ ☐ ☐   Brat Farrar or Come Kill Me
          (1949)

          Thorndike, Russell
☐ ☐ ☐   The Slype (1927)

          Tilton, Alice
          (Phoebe Atwood Taylor)
☐ ☐ ☐   Beginning with a Bash
          (1937)
☐ ☐ ☐   The Cut Direct (1938)
☐ ☐ ☐   Dead Ernest (1944)

- 60 -

Books I:
Have
Read   Want   Own

☐   ☐   ☐   Train, Arthur
                            Tutt and Mr. Tutt (1920)

☐   ☐   ☐   Treat, Lawrence
                            V As in Victim (1945)

☐   ☐   ☐   Trollope, Anthony
                            The Eustace Diamonds
                              (1876)

                        Twain, Mark
☐   ☐   ☐   "The Celebrated Jumping
                            Frog of Calaveras
                            County" (1867)
☐   ☐   ☐   The Tragedy of Pudd'nhead
                            Wilson (1894)

                        Other Books/Notes:

☐   ☐   ☐   _____
☐   ☐   ☐   _____
☐   ☐   ☐   _____
☐   ☐   ☐   _____
☐   ☐   ☐   _____
☐   ☐   ☐   _____
☐   ☐   ☐   _____

Books I:
Have
Read Want own

☐ ☐ ☐ Upfield, Arthur W.
          Murder Down Under or Mr.
            Jelly's Business (1937)
☐ ☐ ☐   The Devil's Steps (1946)

☐ ☐ ☐ Vance, Ethel
          Escape (1939)

☐ ☐ ☐ Vance, Louis Joseph
          The Lone Wolf (1914)

☐ ☐ ☐ Vandercook, John W.
          Murder in Trinidad (1933)

       Van Dine, S.S.
☐ ☐ ☐   The Benson Murder Case
            (1926)
☐ ☐ ☐   The Canary Murder Case
            (1927)
☐ ☐ ☐   The Bishop Murder Case
            (1929)

       Van Gulik, Robert
☐ ☐ ☐   Dee Goong An (1949)

       Vickers, Roy C.
☐ ☐ ☐   The Exploits of Fidelity
            Dove (1924)
☐ ☐ ☐   The Department of Dead
            Ends (1947)

       Vidocq, Francois Eugene
☐ ☐ ☐   Memoirs de Vidocq
            (1828)

Books I:
Have
Read Want Own

☐ ☐ ☐   Wade, Henry
           The Duke of York's Steps
              (1929)
☐ ☐ ☐   Policeman's Lot (1933)
☐ ☐ ☐   Mist on the Saltings
              (1933)
☐ ☐ ☐   Heir Presumptive (1935)

           Wallace, Edgar
☐ ☐ ☐   The Murder Book of Mr.
              J.G. Reeder or The Mind
              of Mr. J.G. Reeder
              (1925)
☐ ☐ ☐   Four Square Jane (1929)

           Walling, R.A.J.
☐ ☐ ☐   The Fatal Five Minutes
              (1932)

           Wallis, J.H.
☐ ☐ ☐   Once Off Guard or The
              Woman in the Window
              (1942)

           Walpole, Sir Hugh
☐ ☐ ☐   Above the Dark Circus
              (1931)

           Walsh, Thomas
☐ ☐ ☐   Nightmare in Manhattan
              (1950)

Books I:
Have
Read Want Own

☐ ☐ ☐ "Waters" (William Russell)
         Recollections of a
         Detective Police-Officer
         or Recollections of a
         Policeman (1852)

☐ ☐ ☐ Wells, Carolyn
         The Clue (1909)

☐ ☐ ☐ Wentworth, Patricia
         The Brading Collection
         (1950)

☐ ☐ ☐ White, Ethel Lina
         The Wheel Spins or The
         Lady Vanishes (1936)

☐ ☐ ☐ Whitechurch, Victor L.
         Thrilling Stories of the
         Railway (1912)

☐ ☐ ☐ Whitfield, Raoul
         Death in a Bowl (1931)

☐ ☐ ☐ Wilde, Oscar
         Lord Arthur Savile's Crime
         and Other Stories (1891)
☐ ☐ ☐   The Picture of Dorian Gray
         (1891)

         Wilde, Percival
☐ ☐ ☐   Rogues in Clover (1929)
☐ ☐ ☐   Inquest (1940)

Books I:
Have
Read Want Own

☐ ☐ ☐ Wilkins, Mary
          The Long Arm (1895)

☐ ☐ ☐ Wilkinson, Ellen
          The Division Bell Mystery
             (1932)

          Williams, Valentine
☐ ☐ ☐   Death Answers the Bell
               (1931)
☐ ☐ ☐   The Portcullis Room (1934)

          Wilson, Mitchell
☐ ☐ ☐   Footsteps Behind Her
               (1941)

          Wilson, P.W.
☐ ☐ ☐   Bride's Castle (1944)

          Woods, Katherine
☐ ☐ ☐   Murder in a Walled Town
               (1934)

          Woodthorpe, R.C.
☐ ☐ ☐   The Public School Murder
               (1932)
☐ ☐ ☐   Rope for a Convict (1940)

          Woolrich, Cornell
          (William Irish)
☐ ☐ ☐   The Bride Wore Black or
               Beware the Lady (1940)
☐ ☐ ☐   Black Alibi (1942)
☐ ☐ ☐   The Black Angel (1943)

Books I: Have Read	Want	Own	
☐	☐	☐	Wylie, Philip Corpses at Indian Stones (1943)
☐	☐	☐	Wynne, Anthony Sinners Go Secretly (1927)
☐	☐	☐	Zangwill, Israel The Big Bow Mystery (1892)

Other Books/Notes:

☐	☐	☐	_____
☐	☐	☐	_____
☐	☐	☐	_____
☐	☐	☐	_____
☐	☐	☐	_____
☐	☐	☐	_____
☐	☐	☐	_____
☐	☐	☐	_____
☐	☐	☐	_____
☐	☐	☐	_____

APPENDIX I

Bookstore Directory

Bookstores

A-1 Crime Fiction
25 Acreman Court
Sherborne, Dorset DT93PW England

Aardvarks Booksellers
Box 15070
Orlando, Florida 32808

The Aspen Bookhouse
Box 4119
Boulder, Colorado 80306

Attic Books
388 Clarence Street
London, Ontario, Canada N6A 3M7
(519) 432-6636

Authors Today Books
1 West California Boulevard
Pasadena, California 91105
(818) 449-9668

Biblioctopus
Idyllwild, California 92349
(714) 659-5188

Big Cat Books
1055 Solano Avenue
Albany, California

Blue Dahlia Bookshop
124 East Beaufort Street
Normal, Illinois 61761
(309) 452-6014

Bookstores/2

Book Baron
1236 South Magnolia Avenue
Anaheim, California 92804
(714) 527-7022

Book Carnival
840 North Tustin Avenue
Orange, California 92667
(714) 538-3210

Bookman's Used Books
2501 East Broadway
Tuscon, Arizona 85716
(602) 325-5767

Bookpress Ltd.
P.O. Box KP
420 Prince George Street
Williamsburg, Virginia 23187
(804) 229-1260

Book Sleuth
2501 West Colorado Avenue
Colorado Springs, Colorado 80904
(303) 632-2727

The Book Stalker
4907 Yaple Avenue
Santa Barbara, California 93111
(805) 964-7601

Bookswappers
1400 Wantagh Avenue
Wantagh, New York 11793
(516) 785-9029

Bookstores/3

Boston Book Annex
906 Beacon Street
Boston, Massachusetts 02215
(617) 266-1090

The Butler Did It
10499A Green Mountain Circle
Columbia, Maryland 21044
(301) 730-1378

Caveat Emptor
108 South Dunn
Bloomington, Indiana 47401
(812) 332-9995

Chaos Unlimited
3506 Connecticut Avenue NW
Washington DC 20008
(202) 244-2710

Chimney Sweep Books
220-A Mount Hermon Road
Scotts Valley, California 95066
(408) 438-1379

Cogitator Books
P.O. Box 405, 344 McKinley
Libertyville, Illinois 60048
(312) 362-4676

Cosmic Enterprises
1200 Hewitt
St. Paul, Minnesota 55104
(612) 644-2566

Bookstores/4

Crime House
175 E. Queen Street
Toronto, Canada M5A 1S2
(416) 365-1338

Crimehouse Mystery Bookstore
112 Avenue Road
Toronto, Ontario M5R 2Y4   Canada

Debra Books
321 Elm Avenue
North Hills, Pennsylvania 19038

Detective-Mystery Books
P.O. Box 15460
Orlando, Florida 32858

Dunn's Mysteries of Choice
251 Baldwin Avenue
Meriden, Connecticut 06450
(203) 235-0480

E. Fithian Books
11502 Telechron Avenue
Whittier, California 90605

Else Fine Books
P.O. Box 43
Dearborn, Michigan 48121
(313) 834-3255

Elsewhere Books
260 Judah Street
San Francisco, California 94122
(415) 661-2535

Bookstores/5

Ergo Books
65 Salisbury Road
Barnet, Herts, England

Escape While There's Still Time
207 East Fifth #105
Eugene, Oregon 97401
(53) 484-9500

Fantasy, Etc.
808 Larkin Street
San Francisco, California 94109
(415) 441-7617

First Impressions
26W580 Butterfield Road
Wheaton, Illinois 60187
(312) 668-9418

Foul Play
10 Eighth Avenue
New York City, New York 10014
(212) 675-5115

    1465-B Second Avenue
    New York City, New York 10021
    (212) 517-3222

Gravesend Books
P.O. Box 235
Pocono Pines, Pennsylvania 18350
(717) 646-3317

Paulette Greene Rare Books
140 Princeton Road
Rockville Centre, New York 11570
(516) 766-8602

Bookstores/6

Grey House Books
12-A Lawrence Street
London SW3, England

Grounds for Murder
Old Town Mercado
2707 Congress Street
San Diego, California 92110
(619) 294-9497

Holm Books
11502 Telechron Avenue
Whittier, California 90605

Hooked on Books
2756 South Campbell
Springfield, Missouri 65807
(417) 882-3397

House of Fiction
663 East Colorado
Pasadena, California 91101
(818) 449-9861

I Love a Mystery
29 East Madison Street
Chicago, Illinois 60602
(312) 236-1338

Janus Books Ltd.
P.O. Box 40787-T
Tuscon, Arizona 85717
(602) 881-8192

Bookstores/7

Joseph the Provider
903 State Street
Santa Barbara, California 93101
(805) 962-6862

Keith and Martin Book Shop
310 West Franklin Stret
Chapel Hill, North Carolina 27514
(919) 942-5178

Key Books
2 West Montgomery Street
Baltimore, Maryland 21230
(301) 539-5020

Limestone Hills Book Shop
P.O. Box 1125
Glen Rose, Texas 76043
(817) 897-4991

Lone Wolf Mystery Bookshop
5705-B Mosholu Avenue
Riverdale, New York 10471
(212) 549-3840

Mainly Mysteries
1300 Raymer Street
North Hollywood, California 91605
(213) 875-0557

Isaac Mendoza Book Co.
15 Ann Street
New York City, New York 10038
(212) 227-8777

Bookstores/8

Mermaid Books
4236-A Piedmont Avenue
Oakland, California 94611
(415) 232-4447

Ming Books
1 Penrose Avenue
Carpenders Park
Watford, Hertfordshire WD1 5AE England

Mitchell Books
1395 East Washington Boulevard
Pasadena, California 91104
(818) 798-4438

Moonstone Bookcellars
2145 Pennsylvania Avenue
Washington D.C., 20037
(202) 659-2600

Mostly Mysteries
225 Carlton Street
Toronto, Ontario M5A 2I2   Canada

Moye, Polley and Brown Booksellers
2231 Second Street
Seattle, Washington
(206) 625-1533

Murder By Mail Mystery Books
600 Mystic Valley Parkway
Suite 295
Medford, Maine 02155

Bookstores/9

Murder By the Book
212 East Cuyahoga Falls Avenue
Akron, Ohio 44310
(216) 434-2112

    1574 South Pearl Street
    Denver, Colorado 80210
    (303) 871-9401

    2348 Bissonnet
    Houston, Texas 77005
    (713) 524-8597

    3729 SE Hawthorn
    Portland, Oregon 97214
    (503) 232-9995

    197 Wickendon Street
    Providence, Rhode Island 02903
    (401) 331-9140

Murder Ink
271 West 87th Street
New York City, New York 10024
(212) 362-8905

Murder Undercover
(Kate's Mystery Books)
2211 Massachusetts Avenue
Cambridge, Massachusetts 02140
(617) 491-2660

Murray's
115 State Street
Springfield, Massachusetts 01101

Bookstores/10

Mysteries from the Yard
616 Xenia Avenue
Yellow Springs, Ohio 45387
(513) 767-2111

The Mysterious Bookshop
129 West 56th Street
New York City, New York 10019
(212) 765-0900

The Mystery Bookstore
2266 North Prospect Avenue #209
Milwaukee, Wisconsin 53202
(414) 277-8515

Mystery Ink
5448 Burnet #7
North Austin, Texas

Mystery Lovers Ink
35 Pelham Road
Salem, New Hampshire 03079

Mystery Manor
P.O. Box 135
Huntington Valley, Pennsylvania 19006
(215) 824-1478

C. Nelson Books
2318 East Third Street
Fremont, Nebraska 68025
(402) 727-1727

Maurice F. Neville Rare Books
835 Laguna Street
Santa Barbara, California
(805) 963-1908

Bookstores/11

North Shore Books Ltd.
8 Green Street
Huntington, New York 11743
(516) 271-5558

Oak Knoll Books
414 Delaware Street
New Castle, Delaware 19720
(302) 328-7232

Oceanside Books
2856 St. John Road
Oceanside, New York 11572

Oliver's Books
16-A Hanover Street
Skowhegan, Maine 04976
(207) 474-9850

Once Upon a Mystery
P.O. Box 590054-A
San Francisco, California 94159

Parnassus Bookstore
Route 6A
Yarmouth Port, Massachusetts 02675
(617) 362-6420

Pepper and Stern
P.O. Box 160
Sharon, Massachusetts 02067
(617) 784-7618

      P.O. Box 2711
      Santa Barbara, California 93120
      (805) 569-0735

Bookstores/12

The Perfect Crime
Gateway Shopping Center
1958 East Sunrise Boulevard
Fort Lauderdale, Florida 33304
(305) 764-2525

The Poisoned Pen
50 First Place
Brooklyn, New York 11231
(718) 596-7739

Prime Crime Books
891 Bank Street
Ottawa, Ontario Canada K1S 3W4

Quest's End
220 The Commons
Ithaca, New York 14850
(607) 272-2221

The Richmond Bookshop
808 West Broad Street
Richmond, Virginia 23220
(804) 644-9970

Rue Morgue
942 Pearl Street
Boulder, Colorado 80302
(303) 443-8346

S & S Books
80 North Wilder
St. Paul, Minnesota 55104
(612) 645-5962

Bookstores/13

San Francisco Mystery Bookstore
746 Diamond Street
San Francisco, California 94114
(415) 282-7444

Savran's Books
301 Cedar Avenue
Minneapolis, Minnesota 55454
(612) 333-0098

Scene of the Crime
13636 Ventura Boulevard
Sherman Oaks, California 91432

Science Fiction & Mystery Bookstore Ltd.
752 1/2 N. Highland NE
Atlanta, Georgia 30306
(404) 975-7326

Anne Sherlock Books
1600-A Bloor Street West
Toronto, Ontario M6P A17 Canada
(416) 533-3207

Sherlock's Home
5614 East Second Street
Long Beach, California 90803
(213) 433-6130

Sherlock in L.A.
2712 Scott Road
Burbank, California 91504

The Silver Door
P.O. Box 3208
Redondo Beach, California 90277
(213) 379-6005

Bookstores/14

John Slattery Books
352 Stanford Avenue
Palo Alto, California 94306
(415) 323-9775

Sleuth of Baker Street
1543 Bayview Avenue
Toronto, Canada M4G 3B5
(416) 483-3111

Marvin Sommer Booksellers
P.O. Box B
Buffalo, New York 14240

Spenser's Mystery Bookshop
314 Newbury Street
Boston, Massachusetts 02115
(617) 262-0880

The Surbiton Book House
8 Victoria Road
Surbiton, Surrey KT64JU England

Sykes and Flanders
P.O. Box 86
Weare, New Hampshire 03281
(603) 529-7432

Sylvester and Orphanos
P.O. Box 2567
Los Angeles, California 90078
(213) 461-1194

Twentieth Century Books
108 King Street
Madison, Wisconsin 53703
(608) 251-6226

Bookstores/15

Uncle Edgar's Mystery Bookstore
2864 Chicago Avenue South
Minneapolis, Minnesota 55407
(612) 874-7575

Used Book Store
474 West Main Street
Kutztown, Pennsylvania 19530
(215) 683-9055

Vagabond Books
2076 Westwood Boulevard
Los Angeles, California 90025
(213) 475-2700

Varney's Volumes
Quaker Ridge Road, P.O. Box 1175, RFD #2
Casco, Maine 04015
(207) 655-4605

Victorian House
East Main Street
Stockton Springs, Maine 04981
(207) 567-3351

Waves Press and Bookshop
4040 MacArthur Avenue
Richmond, Virginia 23227
(804) 264-7276

Whodunit
1931 Chestnut Street
Philadelphia, Pennsylvania 19103
(215) 567-1478

APPENDIX II

25 Easy-to-Find-Favorites

APPENDIX II

25 Easy-to-Find Favorites

If you are new to the mystery genre, you may be at a loss as to where to begin. We have picked 25 favorites from this list as an introduction. If you have problems obtaining any of these books, write to the nearest bookstore listed in Appendix I and it should have no trouble filling your order.

Books I:
Have
Read   Want   Own

[ ]   [ ]   [ ]   Allingham, Margery
                        Death of a Ghost

[ ]   [ ]   [ ]   Beeding, Francis
                        Death Walks in Eastrepps

[ ]   [ ]   [ ]   Blake, Nicholas
                        The Beast Must Die

[ ]   [ ]   [ ]   Cain, James M.
                        Double Indemnity

[ ]   [ ]   [ ]   Chandler, Raymond
                        The Big Sleep

[ ]   [ ]   [ ]   Christie, Agatha
                        The Murder of Roger Ackroyd

[ ]   [ ]   [ ]   Collins, Wilkie
                        The Moonstone

25 Easy-to-Find Favorites/2

Books I:
 Have
 Read Want Own

☐   ☐   ☐   Daly, Elizabeth
                      Arrow Pointing Nowhere

☐   ☐   ☐   Doyle, Sir Arthur Conan
                      A Study in Scarlet

☐   ☐   ☐   Du Maurier, Daphne
                      Rebecca

☐   ☐   ☐   Gardner, Erle Stanley
                      The Case of the Velvet
                      Claws

☐   ☐   ☐   Hammett, Dashiell
                      The Maltese Falcon

☐   ☐   ☐   Highsmith, Patricia
                      Strangers on a Train

☐   ☐   ☐   Iles, Francis
                      Before the Fact

☐   ☐   ☐   Marsh, Ngaio
                      Death in a White Tie

☐   ☐   ☐   McGuire, Paul
                      A Funeral in Eden

☐   ☐   ☐   Orczy, Baroness
                      The Old Man in the Corner

☐   ☐   ☐   Poe, Edgar Allan
                      Tales

25 Easy-to-Find Favorites/3

Books I:
Have
Read Want Own

☐ ☐ ☐ Raymond, Ernest
         We the Accused

☐ ☐ ☐ Sayers, Dorothy L.
         The Nine Tailors

☐ ☐ ☐ Simenon, Georges
         Maigret and the Spinster

☐ ☐ ☐ Stout, Rex
         Some Buried Caesar

☐ ☐ ☐ Symons, Julian
         The Thirty-First of
         February

☐ ☐ ☐ Tey, Josephine
         The Franchise Affair

☐ ☐ ☐ Woolrich, Cornell
         Phantom Lady

APPENDIX III

Coming Attraction:

Please sample our

COMPLETE WORKS OF 70 CRIME WRITERS
SHOPPING LIST

Sample - Complete Works Shopping List

Dorothy L. Sayers

Books I:
Have
Read   Want   Own

☐   ☐   ☐   Whose Body? (1923)
☐   ☐   ☐   Clouds of Witness (1926)
☐   ☐   ☐   Unnatural Death or The Dawson Pedigree (1927)
☐   ☐   ☐   Lord Peter Views the Body (1928)
☐   ☐   ☐   The Unpleasantness at the Bellona Club (1928)
☐   ☐   ☐   The Documents in the Case (1930) [with Robert Eustace]
☐   ☐   ☐   Strong Poison (1930)
☐   ☐   ☐   Five Red Herrings or Suspicious Characters (1931)
☐   ☐   ☐   Have His Carcase (1932)
☐   ☐   ☐   Hangman's Holiday (1933)
☐   ☐   ☐   Murder Must Advertise (1933)
☐   ☐   ☐   The Nine Tailors (1934)
☐   ☐   ☐   Gaudy Night (1935)
☐   ☐   ☐   Busman's Honeymoon (1937)
☐   ☐   ☐   In the Teeth of the Evidence and Other Stories (1939)
☐   ☐   ☐   Striding Folly (1972)

Sample - Complete Works Shopping List

Agatha Christie

Books I:
Have
Read   Want   Own

☐   ☐   ☐   The Mysterious Affair at Styles (1920)
☐   ☐   ☐   The Secret Adversary (1922)
☐   ☐   ☐   The Murder on the Links (1923)
☐   ☐   ☐   The Man in the Brown Suit (1924)
☐   ☐   ☐   Poirot Investigates (1924)
☐   ☐   ☐   The Secret of Chimneys (1925)
☐   ☐   ☐   The Murder of Roger Ackroyd (1926)
☐   ☐   ☐   The Big Four (1927)
☐   ☐   ☐   The Mystery of the Blue Train (1928)
☐   ☐   ☐   The Seven Dials Mystery (1929)
☐   ☐   ☐   Partners in Crime or The Sunningdale Mystery (1929)
☐   ☐   ☐   The Under Dog (1929)
☐   ☐   ☐   The Murder at the Vicarage (1930)
☐   ☐   ☐   The Mysterious Mr. Quin (1930)
☐   ☐   ☐   The Murder at Hazelmoor or The Sittaford Mystery (1931)

Agatha Christie/2

Books I:
Have
Read Want Own

☐ ☐	☐ ☐	☐ ☐	Peril at End House (1932) The Tuesday Club Murders or The Thirteen Problems (1932)
☐	☐	☐	Thirteen at Dinner or Lord Edgeware Dies (1933)
☐	☐	☐	The Hound of Death and Other Stories (1933)
☐	☐	☐	The Boomerang Clue or Why Didn't They Ask Evans? (1934)
☐	☐	☐	Murder on the Orient Express or Murder in the Calais Coach (1934)
☐	☐	☐	Mr. Parker Pyne, Detective or Parker Pyne Investigates (1934)
☐	☐	☐	Murder in Three Acts or Three Act Tragedy (1934)
☐	☐	☐	The Listerdale Mystery and Other Stories (1934)
☐	☐	☐	Death in the Air or Death in the Clouds (1935)
☐	☐	☐	The A.B.C. Murders or The Alphabet Murders (1936)
☐ ☐	☐ ☐	☐ ☐	Cards on the Table (1936) Murder in Mesopotamia (1936)
☐ ☐	☐ ☐	☐ ☐	Death on the Nile (1937) Poirot Loses a Client or Dumb Witness (1937)

Agatha Christie/3

Books I:
 Have
 Read Want Own

  ☐   ☐   ☐   Murder in the Mews and Three Other Poirot Cases or *Dead Man's Mirror and Other Stories* (1937)
  ☐   ☐   ☐   Appointment with Death (1938)
  ☐   ☐   ☐   Murder for Christmas *or A Holiday for Murder;* or Hercule Poirot's Christmas (1938)
  ☐   ☐   ☐   Easy to Kill *or Murder Is Easy* (1939)
  ☐   ☐   ☐   And Then There Were None *or Ten Little Indians;* or *Ten Little Niggers* (1939)
  ☐   ☐   ☐   The Regatta Mystery and Other Stories (1939)
  ☐   ☐   ☐   The Patriotic Murders *or One, Two, Buckle My Shoe;* or *An Overdose of Death* (1940)
  ☐   ☐   ☐   Sad Cypress (1940)
  ☐   ☐   ☐   Evil under the Sun (1941)
  ☐   ☐   ☐   N or M? (1941)
  ☐   ☐   ☐   The Body in the Library (1942)
  ☐   ☐   ☐   The Moving Finger (1942)
  ☐   ☐   ☐   Murder in Retrospect *or Five Little Pigs* (1942)
  ☐   ☐   ☐   The Mystery of the Baghdad Chest (1943)

Agatha Christie/4

Books I:
Have
Read Want Own

☐ ☐ ☐ The Mystery of the Crime in Cabin 66 (1943)
☐ ☐ ☐ Poirot and the Regatta Mystery (1943)
☐ ☐ ☐ Poirot on Holiday (1943)
☐ ☐ ☐ Problem at Pollensa Bay, and Christmas Adventure (1943)
☐ ☐ ☐ The Veiled Lady, and The Mystery of the Baghdad Chest (1944)
☐ ☐ ☐ Death Comes as the End (1944)
☐ ☐ ☐ Towards Zero (1944)
☐ ☐ ☐ Remembered Death or Sparkling Cyanide (1945)
☐ ☐ ☐ Poirot Knows the Murderer (1946)
☐ ☐ ☐ Poirot Lends a Hand (1946)
☐ ☐ ☐ The Hollow or Murder after Hours (1946)
☐ ☐ ☐ The Labours of Hercules (1947)
☐ ☐ ☐ There Is a Tide.... or Taken at the Flood (1948)
☐ ☐ ☐ The Witness for the Prosecution and Other Stories (1948)
☐ ☐ ☐ Crooked House (1949)

Agatha Christie/5

Books I:
Have
Read Want Own

☐ ☐ ☐ Three Blind Mice and Other Stories *or The Mousetrap and Other Stories* (1949)
☐ ☐ ☐ A Murder Is Announced (1950)
☐ ☐ ☐ They Came to Baghdad (1951)
☐ ☐ ☐ The Under Dog and Other Stories (1951)
☐ ☐ ☐ Th Mousetrap (1952)
☐ ☐ ☐ Murder with Mirrors *or They Do It with Mirrors* (1952)
☐ ☐ ☐ Mrs. McGinty's Dead *or Blood Will Tell* (1952)
☐ ☐ ☐ Funerals Are Fatal *or After the Funeral; or Murder at the Gallop* (1953)
☐ ☐ ☐ A Pocket Full of Rye (1953)
☐ ☐ ☐ So Many Steps to Death *or Destination Unknown* (1954)
☐ ☐ ☐ Hickory, Dickory, Death *or Hickory, Dickory, Dock* (1955)
☐ ☐ ☐ Dead Man's Folly (1956)
☐ ☐ ☐ What Mrs. McGillicuddy Saw! *or 4:50 from Paddington; or Murder She Said* (1957)
☐ ☐ ☐ Ordeal by Innocence (1958)
☐ ☐ ☐ Cat among the Pigeons (1959)

Agatha Christie/6

Have Read	Want	Own	
☐	☐	☐	The Adventure of the Christmas Pudding, and Selection of Entrees (1960)
☐	☐	☐	Double Sin ad Other Stories (1961)
☐	☐	☐	The Pale Horse (1961)
☐	☐	☐	The Mirror Crack'd or The Mirror Crack'd from Side to Side (1962)
☐	☐	☐	The Clocks (1963)
☐	☐	☐	A Caribbean Mystery (1964)
☐	☐	☐	At Bertram's Hotel (1965)
☐	☐	☐	Third Girl (1966)
☐	☐	☐	13 Clues for Miss Marple (1966)
☐	☐	☐	Endless Night (1967)
☐	☐	☐	By the Pricking of My Thumbs (1968)
☐	☐	☐	Hallowe'en Party (1969)
☐	☐	☐	Passenger to Frankfurt (1970)
☐	☐	☐	Nemesis (1971)
☐	☐	☐	The Golden Ball and Other Stories (1971)
☐	☐	☐	Elephants Can Remember (1972)
☐	☐	☐	Postern of Fate (1973)
☐	☐	☐	Hercule Poirot's Early Cases or Poirot's Early Cases (1974)

Agatha Christie/7

Books I:
 Have
 Read Want Own

  ☐   ☐   ☐   Curtain: Hercule Poirot's
                  Last Case (1975)
  ☐   ☐   ☐   Sleeping Murder (1976)
  ☐   ☐   ☐   The Mousetrap and Other
                  Plays (1978) [includes
                  Witness for the
                  Prosecution, Ten Little
                  Indians, Appointment
                  with Death, The Hollow,
                  Towards Zero, Verdict,
                  and Go Back for Murder]
  ☐   ☐   ☐   Miss Marple's Final Cases
                  and Two Other Stories
                  (1979)

The Complete Works of 70 Crime Writers Shopping List will be available October 1st, 1986.

This book should be available at all mystery bookshops, but if you have difficulty finding a copy, you can order one by post. Please fill in the form below.

NAME _____

ADDRESS _____

_____

_____

Enclose a check or money order payable to Pamela Granovetter at The Copperfield Press, 306 West 11th Street, New York City, New York 10014 in the amount of $5.00 per copy. Please add 35¢ per copy for postage. New York residents please add sales tax.

SPECIAL: For every 5 copies ordered, you will receive one free, and postage will be on us.

Offer good through July 1, 1987.